T0109815

erTip

The Great Depression

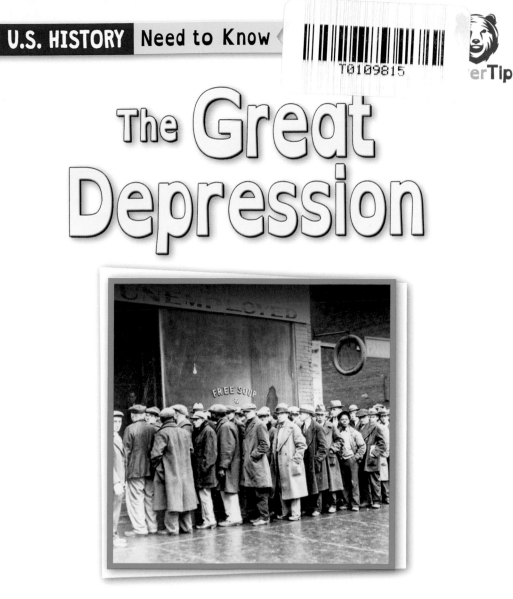

by Karen Latchana Kenney

Consultant: Caitlin Krieck
Social Studies Teacher and Instructional Coach
The Lab School of Washington

BEARPORT PUBLISHING

Minneapolis, Minnesota

Credits

Cover and title page, © U.S. National Archives and Records Administration/Wikimedia Creative Commons license 3.0; 5, © Everett Collection/Shutterstock; 7, © DEA PICTURE LIBRARY/Getty Images; 8–9, © LC-USZ62–123429/Library of Congress; 11, © Scherl/Süddeutsche Zeitung Photo/Alamy; 15, © Corbis Historical/Getty Images; 17, © Popperfoto/Getty Images; 19, © LC-H21- C-74/Library of Congress; 20, © Victor Maschek/Shutterstock; 21, © RBM Vintage Images/Alamy; 23, © LC-USF34-004051-E/Library of Congress; 25, © LC-H21- C-612/Library of Congress; 27, © f11photo/Shutterstock; and 28, © LC-USZ62-75787/Library of Congress.

Bearport Publishing Company Product Development Team

President: Jen Jenson; Director of Product Development: Spencer Brinker; Managing Editor: Allison Juda; Associate Editor: Naomi Reich; Associate Editor: Tiana Tran, Senior Designer: Colin O'Dea; Associate Designer: Elena Klinkner; Associate Designer: Kayla Eggert; Product Development Specialist: Anita Stasson

A NOTE FROM THE PUBLISHER: Some of the historic photos in this book have been colorized to help readers have a more meaningful and rich experience. The color results are not intended to depict actual historical detail.

Library of Congress Cataloging-in-Publication Data

Names: Kenney, Karen Latchana, author.
Title: The Great Depression / by Karen Latchana Kenney.
Description: Minneapolis, Minnesota : Bearport Publishing Company, [2024] | Series: U.S. history: need to know | "SilverTip." | Includes bibliographical references and index.
Identifiers: LCCN 2023006116 (print) | LCCN 2023006117 (ebook) | ISBN 9798888220306 (library binding) | ISBN 9798888222218 (paperback) | ISBN 9798888223451 (ebook)
Subjects: LCSH: United States—History—1933-1945—Juvenile literature. | United States—History—1919-1933—Juvenile literature. | Depressions, 1929—United States—Juvenile literature. | New Deal, 1933-1939—Juvenile literature. | United States—Economic conditions—1918-1945—Juvenile literature.
Classification: LCC E806 .K425 2024 (print) | LCC E806 (ebook) | DDC 973.916—dc23/eng/20230214
LC record available at https://lccn.loc.gov/2023006116
LC ebook record available at https://lccn.loc.gov/2023006117

For more information, write to Bearport Publishing, 5357 Penn Avenue South, Minneapolis, MN 55419.

Contents

Waiting for Food

Hundreds joined the line that stretched for blocks. These people were hungry and broke. At **breadlines** like this they could get free soup and coffee.

During the Great Depression, many people lost their jobs. They faced **poverty**. What caused these difficult times?

Breadlines and soup kitchens could be found across the United States during the 1930s. Many were run by charities. At the time, government programs did not offer free food to people in need.

Stocks Take a Turn

During the 1920s, the **economy** was doing well. Most people who wanted jobs had them. This meant people had money to spend.

The **stock market** was growing, too. It gave average people the chance to get rich quickly. Many did not see the risks ahead.

Many companies sell stocks, or parts of their business. People can buy them through the stock market. When stock prices rise, stocks have more value. Stock owners make money. When stock prices fall, people lose money.

The stock market is in New York City.

In October 1929, the stock market changed. People started to lose money. So, they wanted to get out of the market fast. This made matters worse. The more that people sold stocks, the less value stocks had. Soon, the market crashed. This was the start of the Great Depression.

The stock market crash impacted many average Americans. People lost their life savings in a day. Many didn't have much to begin with. They had sunk all their money into stocks.

PASSPORT PHOTOS 10

CAUTION
SPEED LIMIT 8 MILES PER HOUR
AXLE LOAD RESTRICTED TO 10 TONS

People gathered outside the stock market as it crashed.

Money Mania

Panic after the crash further hurt the economy. Many people wanted to hang on to what little money they had left. They stopped buying as many things. So, factories stopped making as much. Workers lost their jobs. The **unemployment rate** rose. Those who kept their jobs were paid less than before.

The Great Depression was felt around the world. Countries in Europe, South America, and Asia also went into a depression. Unemployment rates rose there, too. Their money lost value.

Unemployed workers

Suddenly, people did not trust that their money was safe. They rushed to their banks. During these bank panics, many people demanded their money back. Soon, banks had nothing left. They started going **bankrupt**. The banks could not pay their debts or employees. So, they shut down.

There were four major bank panics during the 1930s. Many people lost all their money. Throughout the Depression, around 9,000 banks across the country failed.

Failing Farms

Soon, life became hard for farmers, too. A severe **drought** made farms across the middle of the country fail. Crops died. Winds blew away the dry soil and started huge dust storms. They killed people and animals and damaged much in their path. This came to be known as the **Dust Bowl**.

Thousands of farmers left their farms after the Dust Bowl. Many were from Oklahoma. They moved west to California to find work. People called this the Okie Migration.

Dust storms clouded the skies during the Dust Bowl.

Desperate for Food

After farms failed, there was less food. At the same time, people were out of money and started losing their homes. Many could not afford food, even if they could find it.

Food **riots** broke out. Across the country, people smashed grocery store windows and took anything they could get.

People without homes moved into large **shantytowns**. Some people made shacks out of wood, tin, and cardboard. Many lived in tents. Often, their only options for food were soup kitchens and breadlines.

A food riot in 1931

The New Deal

Americans needed a change. In 1932, they elected Franklin D. Roosevelt president. He promised to help turn things around.

Right away, Roosevelt started a series of government programs. He called them the New Deal. New Deal laws helped banks so people could keep their money safe.

Roosevelt knew people were afraid and worried. He gave speeches over the radio. These talks came to be known as fireside chats. The president used them to help calm everyone.

Roosevelt took office on March 4, 1933.

Some New Deal programs gave people work and money. The Works Progress Administration created jobs. Its workers built schools, hospitals, and roads. The Social Security Administration paid people still without jobs. It gave money to older people and those who could not work, too.

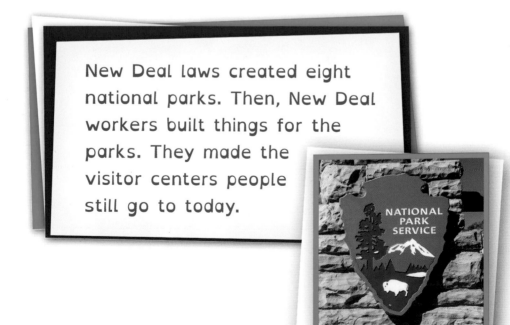

New Deal laws created eight national parks. Then, New Deal workers built things for the parks. They made the visitor centers people still go to today.

NATIONAL PARK SERVICE

Helping the Land

After the Dust Bowl, the land needed **protection**. Harmful farming practices were a big cause of the disaster. So, programs taught farmers how to protect the soil. They helped farmers take care of their land.

Workers planted trees, too. This stopped wind from blowing soil into the air.

Farmers started using cover crops. These plants aren't grown to be eaten. Instead, they are planted because their roots help keep soil in place.

Slow Recovery

It would take a while to see the full effects of the New Deal. For years, the economy continued to go up and down. The government did what it could to try and level it out. By 1939, the Great Depression was over.

People liked Roosevelt's New Deal programs. They kept voting him into office. Roosevelt was elected president four times. This was the most of any U.S. president.

Lasting Effects

The Great Depression reshaped America. Many laws and policies created during that time are still in place. They provide safety nets for people who lose their jobs. New Deal agencies continue to protect the land, too. These efforts help Americans to this day.

Many government agencies that started during the New Deal protected people's money. One made new rules to try and make the stock market safer. It is still around today.

Without Work

One of the biggest problems during the Great Depression was the loss of jobs. See the unemployment rate before, during, and immediately after the Great Depression.

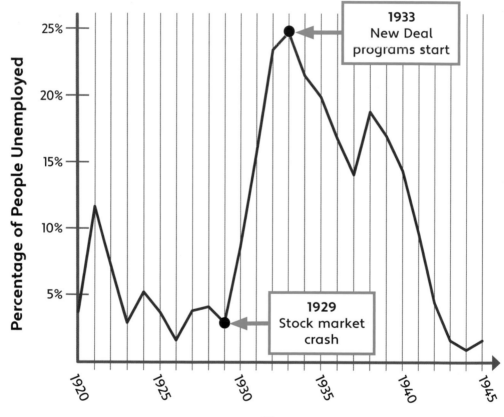

Percentage of People Unemployed

1933
New Deal programs start

1929
Stock market crash

Year

★ SilverTips for REVIEW

Review what you've learned. Use the text to help you.

Define key terms

Dust Bowl

economy

New Deal

stock market

unemployment

Check for understanding

How did the Great Depression start?

Why did bank panics make the Great Depression worse?

Explain how dust storms impacted different people during the Great Depression.

Think deeper

How do you think New Deal programs affected workers immediately following the Great Depression? What are their longstanding impacts today?

★ SilverTips on TEST-TAKING

- **Make a study plan.** Ask your teacher what the test is going to cover. Then, set aside time to study a little bit every day.

- **Read all the questions carefully.** Be sure you know what is being asked.

- **Skip any questions** you don't know how to answer right away. Mark them and come back later if you have time.

Glossary

bankrupt made unable to pay debts

breadlines lines of people waiting to receive free food

drought a long period of time when there is very little or no rain

economy the system of buying, selling, making things, and managing money in a place

poverty the state of being very poor

protection something that keeps something or someone safe from harm

riots out-of-control actions taken by crowds

shantytowns areas of town with small structures made of found materials, such as wood and cardboard

stock market a place where people can buy and sell parts of companies

unemployment rate the amount of people who do not have jobs given as a percentage of the population

Read More

Gitlin, Martin. *The Great Depression (American Eras: Defining Moments).* Ann Arbor, MI: Cherry Lake Publishing, 2022.

London, Martha. *Franklin D. Roosevelt (Influential Presidents).* Lake Elmo, MN: Focus Readers, 2023.

Smith, Elliott. *Focus on the Great Depression (History in Pictures).* Minneapolis: Lerner Publications, 2023.

Learn More Online

1. Go to **www.factsurfer.com** or scan the QR code below.

2. Enter "**Great Depression**" into the search box.

3. Click on the cover of this book to see a list of websites.

Index

About the Author

Karen Latchana Kenney is an author in Minnetonka, Minnesota. She enjoys writing about important moments in history.